Word Family

Creative Activities
for Literacy

Written and Illustrated by
Sandy Baker

Frank Schaffer Publications®

Author: Sandy Baker
Illustrator: Sandy Baker
Editor: Karen Thompson

Frank Schaffer Publications®

Send all inquiries to:
Frank Schaffer Publications
8720 Orion Place
Columbus, Ohio 43240-2111

Word Family DoodleLoops

ISBN: 0-7682-3369-0

1 2 3 4 5 6 7 8 9 10 MAZ 12 11 10 09 08 07

Table of Contents

Published by Frank Schaffer Publications. Copyright protected.   0-7682-3369-0 *Word Family DoodleLoops*

A Word About *Word Family DoodleLoops*

Directions for Teaching *Word Family DoodleLoops*

The activities in *Word Family DoodleLoops* are unique learning tools that offer meaningful and stimulating ways to introduce or practice word families—words with similar sounds and letter patterns. Writing, reading and experiencing these words is an effective way to teach decoding skills to emergent readers.

Word Family DoodleLoops introduces 21 different word families that have been identified as common phonograms comprising high-frequency words. Each word family is presented on two consecutive pages. On the first, students fill in letters to complete all words in the family. Then they identify pictures by correctly spelling the word that describes each picture.

On the second page, students follow a series of directions and complete drawings based on those directions. One or more of the words in the word family is included in each sentence of the directions. For example, if students are learning or practicing words in the ad family, the directions may read:

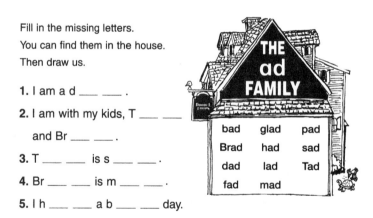

Try to spend at least two sessions on each word family included in *Word Family DoodleLoops*. Introduce word families by distributing copies of the first word family activity. You may wish to illustrate this page on the chalkboard or display it using an overhead projector.

These activities may be used as a cooperative learning tool by encouraging two or three students to work together. As an assessment tool or a portfolio piece, these completed activities will give a good indication of a student's development.

Directions for Teaching *Word Family DoodleLoops* Continued

Phonemic Awareness: Introduce the name of the word family and discuss the sounds of the letters. For example, if you are introducing the ad family, explain that each word in this family is spelled with an a-d at the end. The vowel a has a short a sound. Give a pronunciation of the letters and have the students practice this sound. Instruct students to look for the beginning letter or letters of each word written on the house. As a whole group, sound out these beginning letters separately.

Phonics: Add the letters a and d to complete each word. Say the words individually, sounding out each letter or blend until each word is complete. When the ad of each word is sounded out, it is best to sound out the letters separately, and then together. Invite students to fill in the words in the house.

Vocabulary: Encourage students to take turns reading the words they have created. As each student reads the words, fill them in on the chalkboard or overhead. Ask students if they know what each word means or refers to, and give a brief definition of each. Each word may be added to a word list, a word wall, or individual word banks if desired.

Reading: Have students think of additional words that end with the same word family. List these words as well. Direct students' attention to the pictures surrounding the word family house. Ask students to find the word in the house that best describes each picture. Encourage students to write the words in the spaces provided next to each picture. Help students choose correct words for each picture the first time they tackle a word family by working with them on the chalkboard or overhead. Read the words that have been created.

DoodleLoops

Fill in the missing letters in the *ack* family.
Then label the pictures.

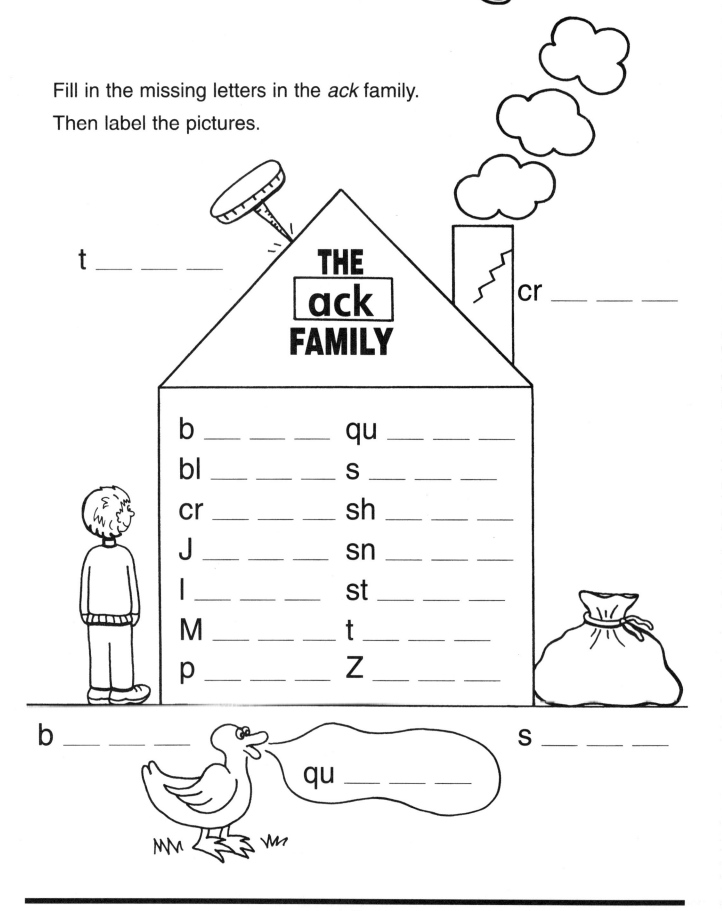

t _ _ _ _

cr _ _ _ _

**THE
ack
FAMILY**

b _ _ _ _   qu _ _ _ _

bl _ _ _ _   s _ _ _ _

cr _ _ _ _   sh _ _ _ _

J _ _ _ _   sn _ _ _ _

l _ _ _ _   st _ _ _ _

M _ _ _ _   t _ _ _ _

p _ _ _ _   Z _ _ _ _

b _ _ _ _

qu _ _ _ _

s _ _ _ _

0-7682-3369-0 *Word Family DoodleLoops*

DoodleLoops

Fill in the missing letters.
You can find them in the house.
Then draw us.

THE ack FAMILY

back	Mack	shack
black	pack	snack
crack	quack	stack
Jack	rack	tack
lack	sack	Zack

1. I am J ___ ___ ___ .

2. I have a b ___ ___ ___

    p ___ ___ ___ .

3. My hair is bl ___ ___ ___ .

4. I am eating a sn ___ ___ ___ .

5. I am with my twin M ___ ___ ___ .

Published by Frank Schaffer Publications. Copyright protected.   0-7682-3369-0 *Word Family DoodleLoops*

DoodleLoops

Fill in the missing letters in the *ad* family.
Then label the pictures.

Br __ __ is gl __ __

THE
ad
FAMILY

b __ __   l __ __
Br __ __ __   m __ __
d __ __   p __ __
f __ __   s __ __
gl __ __   T __ __
h __ __

D __ __   is s __ __   T __ __   is m __ __

8

0-7682-3369-0   *Word Family DoodleLoops*

DoodleLoops

Fill in the missing letters.
You can find them in the house.
Then draw us.

1. I am a d ___ ___ .

2. I am with my kids, T ___ ___

and Br ___ ___ .

3. T ___ ___ is s ___ ___ .

4. Br ___ ___ is m ___ ___ .

5. I h ___ ___ a b ___ ___ day!

THE ad FAMILY

bad	glad	pad
Brad	had	sad
dad	lad	Tad
fad	mad	

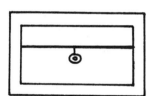

DoodleLoops

Fill in the missing letters in the *ail* family.

Then label the pictures.

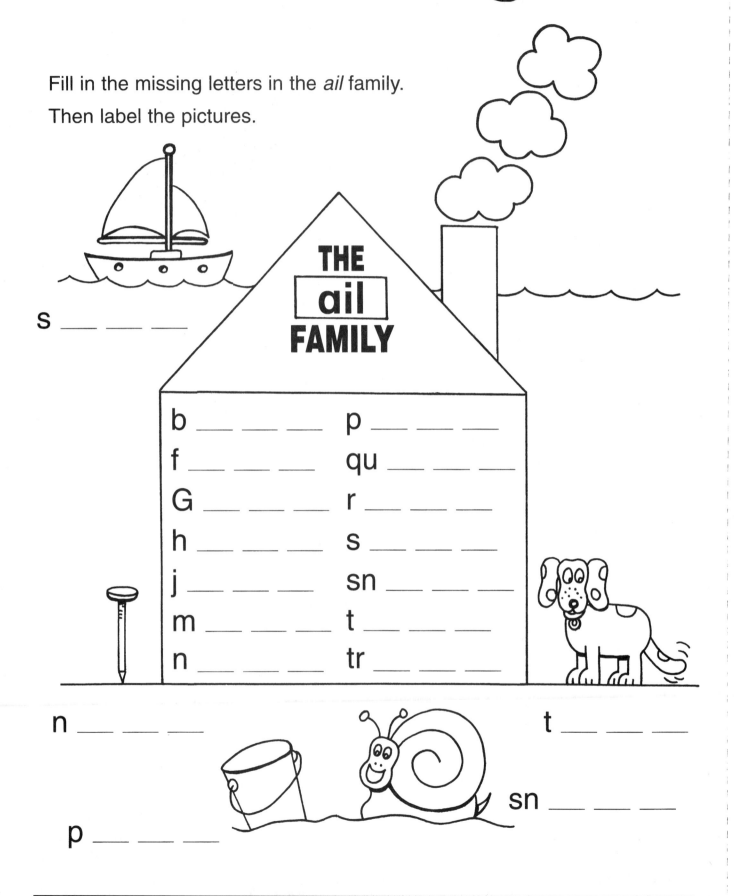

s _ _ _ _

THE | **ail** | **FAMILY**

b _ _ _ _   p _ _ _ _
f _ _ _ _   qu _ _ _ _
G _ _ _ _   r _ _ _ _
h _ _ _ _   s _ _ _ _
j _ _ _ _   sn _ _ _ _
m _ _ _ _   t _ _ _ _
n _ _ _ _   tr _ _ _ _

n _ _ _ _   t _ _ _ _

sn _ _ _ _

p _ _ _ _

0-7682-3369-0   *Word Family DoodleLoops*

DoodleLoops

Fill in the missing letters.
You can find them in the house.
Then draw me.

1. I am G ___ ___ ___ .

2. I am walking on a

tr ___ ___ ___ .

3. I have a p ___ ___ ___ .

4. I just found a sn ___ ___ ___ .

5. It is starting to h ___ ___ ___ .

THE
ail
FAMILY

DOODLE
LOOPS

bail	mail	sail
fail	nail	snail
Gail	pail	tail
hail	quail	trail
jail	rail	

DoodleLoops

Fill in the missing letters in the *ain* family.

Then label the pictures.

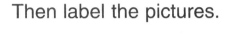

tr _ _ _ _

THE
ain
FAMILY

r _ _ _ _

br_ _ _ _   p_ _ _ _

ch_ _ _ _   pl_ _ _ _

dr_ _ _ _   r_ _ _ _

g_ _ _ _   st_ _ _ _

gr_ _ _ _   str_ _ _ _

m_ _ _ _   tr_ _ _ _

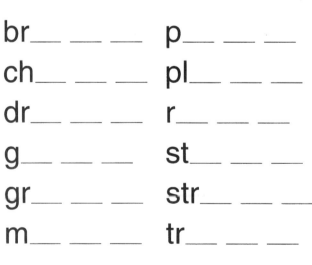

br _ _ _ _   ch _ _ _ _

DoodleLoops

Fill in the missing letters.
You can find them in the house.
Then draw me.

1. I am in the r ___ ___ ___ .

2. I am on M ___ ___ ___

Street .

3. I am wearing a ch ___ ___ ___ .

4. The ch ___ ___ ___ gives

me a p ___ ___ ___ .

5. I can see a tr ___ ___ ___ .

THE
ain
FAMILY

DOODLE
LOOPS

brain	grain	rain
chain	Main	stain
drain	pain	strain
gain	plain	train

Main
Street

Published by Frank Schaffer Publications. Copyright protected.   0-7682-3369-0 *Word Family DoodleLoops*

DoodleLoops

Fill in the missing letters in the *ake* family.

Then label the pictures.

THE **ake** **FAMILY**

l _ _ _ _

b_ _ _ _   qu_ _ _ _

br_ _ _ _   r_ _ _ _

c_ _ _ _   s_ _ _ _

dr_ _ _ _   sh_ _ _ _

f_ _ _ _   sn_ _ _ _

fl_ _ _ _   st_ _ _ _

J_ _ _ _   t_ _ _ _

l_ _ _ _   w_ _ _ _

m_ _ _ _

r _ _ _ _

c _ _ _ _

sn _ _ _ _

0-7682-3369-0 *Word Family DoodleLoops*

DoodleLoops

Fill in the missing letters.
You can find them in the house.
Then draw us.

1. My name is J ___ ___ ___ .

2. I am with my pet

sn ___ ___ ___ .

3. We both like to b ___ ___ ___ .

4. We just made a c ___ ___ ___ .

5. We are eating it by a

l ___ ___ ___ .

THE
ake
FAMILY

bake	Jake	shake
brake	lake	snake
cake	make	stake
drake	quake	take
fake	rake	wake
flake	sake	

0-7682-3369-0 *Word Family DoodleLoops*

Fill in the missing letters in the *an* family.

Then label the pictures.

J ___ ___

p ___ ___ ___

THE
an
FAMILY

m ___ ___ ___

br ___ ___	p ___ ___ ___
c ___ ___ ___	r ___ ___ ___
D ___ ___	St ___ ___ ___
f ___ ___ ___	t ___ ___
J ___ ___ ___	th ___ ___ ___
m ___ ___ ___	v ___ ___
N ___ ___ ___	

f ___ ___ ___

c ___ ___ ___

DoodleLoops

Fill in the missing letters.
You can find them in the house.
Then draw us.

1. I am a m ___ ___ .

2. My name is St ___ ___ .

3. I am in a v ___ ___ .

4. The v ___ ___ is t ___ ___ .

5. I see my friends D ___ ___

   and Fr___ ___ .

THE
an
FAMILY

DoodlE LOOPS

bran	Jan	Stan
can	man	tan
Dan	Nan	than
fan	pan	van
Fran	ran	

DoodleLoops

Fill in the missing letters in the *at* family.

Then label the pictures.

b _ _

THE
at
FAMILY

h _ _

b _ _	m _ _
br _ _	P _ _
c _ _	r _ _
ch _ _	s _ _
f _ _	sc _ _
fl _ _	th _ _
h _ _	v _ _

c _ _

WELCOME

P _ _

m _ _

0-7682-3369-0 *Word Family DoodleLoops*

DoodleLoops

Fill in the missing letters.

You can find them in the house.

Then draw me.

THE at FAMILY

bat	flat	sat
brat	hat	scat
cat	mat	that
chat	Pat	vat
fat	rat	

1. My name is P___ ___ .

2. I am a f___ ___ c___ ___ .

3. I have a b___ ___ .

4. I s___ ___ on a m___ ___ .

5. I am wearing a funny h___ ___ .

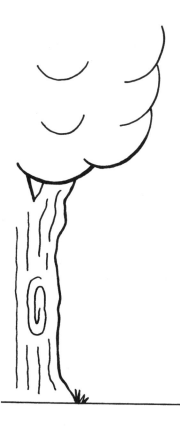

DoodleLoops

Fill in the missing letters in the *ay* family.

Then label the pictures.

j _ _

K _ _ _

spr _ _ _

THE

ay

FAMILY

aw _ _	m _ _ _
b _ _ _	p _ _ _
cl _ _ _	pl _ _ _
d _ _ _	pr _ _ _
F _ _ _	R _ _
g _ _ _	s _ _ _
gr _ _ _	spr _ _ _
h _ _ _	st _ _ _
J _ _ _	str _ _ _
K _ _ _	tr _ _ _
l _ _ _	w _ _ _

h _ _

tr _ _ _

0-7682-3369-0 *Word Family DoodleLoops*

DoodleLoops

Fill in the missing letters.
You can find them in the house.
Then draw us.

THE ay FAMILY

DoodleLoops

away	hay	Ray
bay	Jay	say
clay	Kay	spray
day	lay	stay
Fay	may	stray
gay	pay	tray
gray	play	way
	pray	

1. We are F ___ ___

and K ___ ___ .

2. We like to pl ___ ___ .

3. We pl ___ ___ with cl ___ ___ .

4. The cl ___ ___ is on

a tr ___ ___ .

5. The cl ___ ___ is gr ___ ___ .

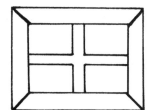
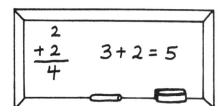

$$\begin{array}{r} 2 \\ +\,2 \\ \hline 4 \end{array}$$ $3 + 2 = 5$

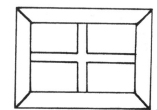

DoodleLoops

Fill in the missing letters in the *eed* family.

Then label the pictures.

w _____ _____ _____

THE
eed
FAMILY

Ouch!

Mmmm!

bl _____ _____ _____   ind _____ _____ _____   bl _____ _____ _____
br _____ _____ _____   n _____ _____ _____
d _____ _____ _____   s _____ _____ _____
f _____ _____ _____   sp _____ _____ _____
gr _____ _____ _____   w _____ _____ _____
h _____ _____ _____

f _____ _____ _____

s _____ _____ _____

DoodleLoops

Fill in the missing letters.
You can find them in the house.
Then draw my plant and me.

THE eed FAMILY

bleed	greed	seed
breed	heed	speed
deed	indeed	weed
feed	need	

1. I plant a s ___ ___ ___ .

2. I f ___ ___ ___ my

    s ___ ___ ___ .

3. Then I w ___ ___ ___ .

4. It grows so big, ind ___ ___ ___ !

5. What a strange br ___ ___ ___ !

DoodleLoops

Fill in the missing letters in the *ell* family.

Then label the pictures.

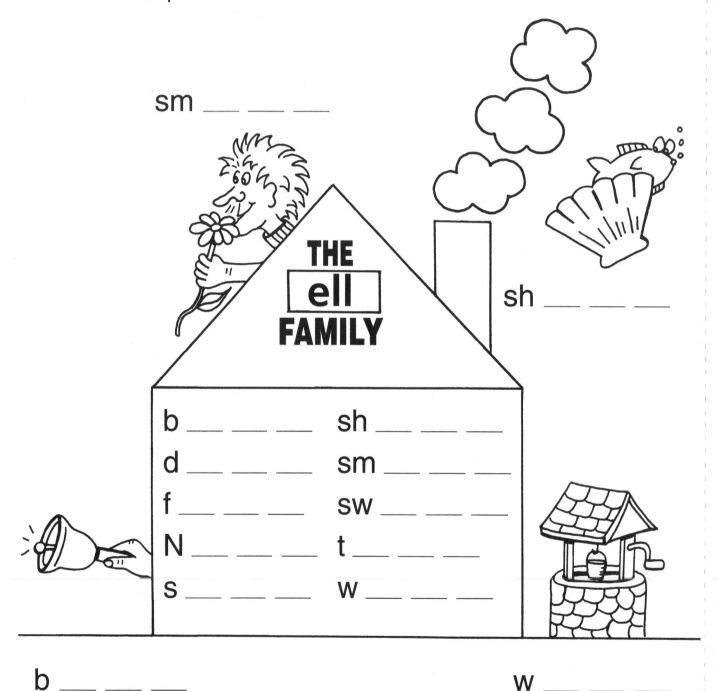

sm ___ ___ ___

sh ___ ___ ___

THE
ell
FAMILY

b ___ ___ ___	sh ___ ___ ___
d ___ ___ ___	sm ___ ___ ___
f ___ ___ ___	sw ___ ___ ___
N ___ ___ ___	t ___ ___ ___
s ___ ___ ___	w ___ ___ ___

b ___ ___ ___

w ___ ___ ___

DoodleLoops

Fill in the missing letters.

You can find them in the house.

Then draw me.

1. I am N ___ ___ ___ .

2. I just f ___ ___ ___ .

3. I don't feel w ___ ___ ___ .

4. My foot is starting to

sw ___ ___ ___ .

5. Don't t ___ ___ ___ my mom!

THE ell FAMILY

bell	Nell	swell
dell	sell	tell
fell	shell	well
	smell	

DoodleLoops

Fill in the missing letters in the *ew* family.

Then label the pictures.

fl __ __ __

THE **ew** **FAMILY**

bl __ __ __   gr __ __ __

br __ __ __   kn __ __ __

ch __ __ __   m __ __ __

cr __ __ __   n __ __ __

d __ __ __   scr __ __ __

dr __ __ __   st __ __ __

f __ __ __   vi __ __ __

fl __ __ __

m __ __ __

scr __ __ __

0-7682-3369-0 *Word Family DoodleLoops*

DoodleLoops

Fill in the missing letters.
You can find them in the house.
Then draw the crew, the spaceship,
and the alien plants.

THE ew FAMILY

blew	drew	mew
brew	few	new
chew	flew	screw
crew	grew	stew
dew	knew	view

1. We are a UFO cr ___ ___ .

2. We just fl ___ ___ to Earth.

3. Our spaceship is n ___ ___ .

4. We planted a f ___ ___

alien seeds.

5. They gr ___ ___ and gr___ ___ .

DoodleLoops

Fill in the missing letters in the *ick* family.

Then label the pictures.

l _ _ _

THE
ick
FAMILY

br _ _ _ _   qu _ _ _ _

ch _ _ _ _   R _ _ _ _

cl _ _ _ _   s _ _ _ _

D _ _ _ _   sl _ _ _ _

k _ _ _ _   st _ _ _ _

l _ _ _ _   t _ _ _ _

M _ _ _ _   th _ _ _ _

N _ _ _ _   w _ _ _ _

p _ _ _ _

Peep!

ch _ _ _   s _ _ _

st _ _ _

0-7682-3369-0 *Word Family DoodleLoops*

DoodleLoops

Fill in the missing letters.
You can find them in the house.
Then draw Nick, Dick, and Rick.

THE ick FAMILY

brick	Mick	slick
chick	Nick	stick
click	pick	thick
Dick	quick	tick
kick	Rick	wick
lick	sick	

1. N ___ ___ ___ plays football.

2. He will k ___ ___ ___ the ball.

3. He kicks it to D ___ ___ ___ .

4. D ___ ___ ___ passes to R ___ ___ ___ .

5. R ___ ___ ___ is qu ___ ___ ___ !

0-7682-3369-0 *Word Family DoodleLoops*

DoodleLoops

Fill in the missing letters in the *ight* family.

Then label the pictures.

br __ __ __ __

l __ __ __ __

THE
ight
FAMILY

fr _____ __

br _____ __   n _____ __

f _____ __   r _____ __

fr _____ __   s _____ __

l _____ __   sl _____ __

m _____ __   t _____ __

f __ __ __ __

DoodleLoops

Fill in the missing letters.
You can find them in the house.
Then draw the strange sight.

THE
ight
FAMILY

bright	light	sight
fight	might	slight
fright	night	tight
	right	

1. It is n ___ ___ ___ ___ .

2. I see a strange

s ___ ___ ___ ___ .

3. It is very br ___ ___ ___ ___ .

4. It makes the sky

l ___ ___ ___ ___ .

5. It gives me a fr ___ ___ ___ ___ .

0-7682-3369-0 *Word Family DoodleLoops*

DoodleLoops

Fill in the missing letters in the *ill* family.

Then label the pictures.

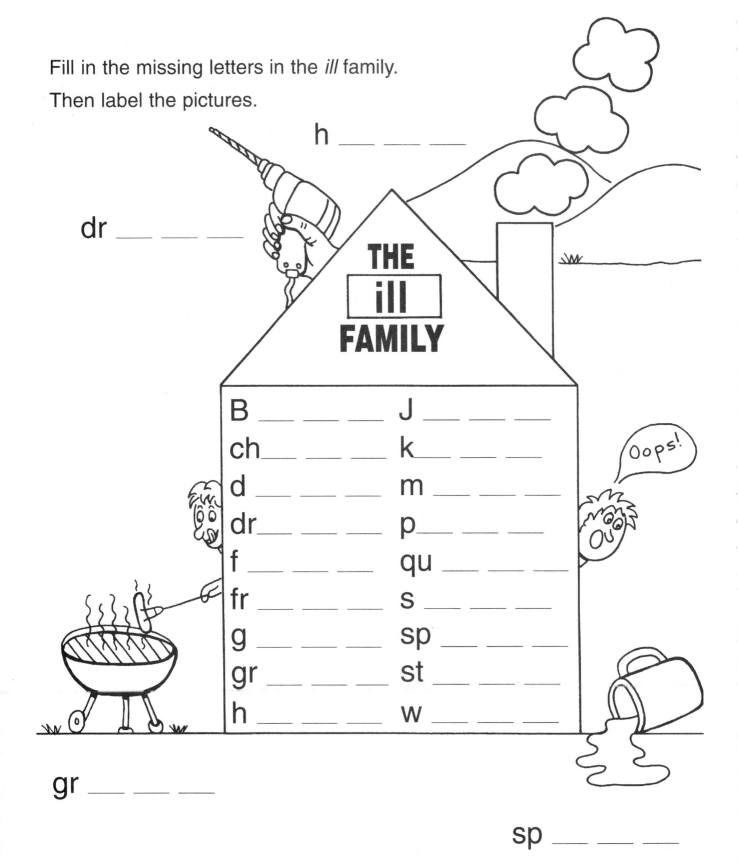

h _____ _____ _____

dr _____ _____ _____

**THE
ill
FAMILY**

B _____ _____ _____	J _____ _____ _____
ch _____ _____ _____	k _____ _____ _____
d _____ _____ _____	m _____ _____ _____
dr _____ _____ _____	p _____ _____ _____
f _____ _____ _____	qu _____ _____ _____
fr _____ _____ _____	s _____ _____ _____
g _____ _____ _____	sp _____ _____ _____
gr _____ _____ _____	st _____ _____ _____
h _____ _____ _____	w _____ _____ _____

Oops!

gr _____ _____ _____ _____

sp _____ _____ _____

Published by Frank Schaffer Publications. Copyright protected.

0-7682-3369-0 *Word Family DoodleLoops*

DoodleLoops

Fill in the missing letters.
You can find them in the house.
Then draw me and Jill.

1. I am B ___ ___ ___ .

2. I am feeling ___ ___ ___ .

3. I have a ch ___ ___ ___ .

4. J ___ ___ ___ is giving

me a p ___ ___ ___ .

5. I w ___ ___ ___ lie

st ___ ___ ___ .

THE
ill
FAMILY

Bill	gill	pill
chill	grill	quill
dill	hill	sill
drill	ill	spill
fill	Jill	still
frill	kill	will
	mill	

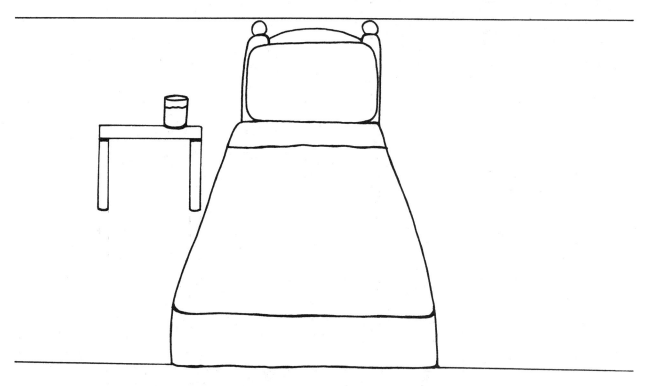

DoodleLoops

Fill in the missing letters in the *ine* family.

Then label the pictures.

l _ _ _ _

w _ _ _ _

THE
ine
FAMILY

d _ _ _ _ _   n _ _ _ _ _

div _ _ _ _ _   p _ _ _ _ _

f _ _ _ _   v _ _ _ _

l _ _ _ _   wh _ _ _ _

m _ _ _ _   w _ _ _ _

9

v _ _ _ _

n _ _ _ _

Fill in the missing letters.

You can find them in the house.

Then draw us.

1. We d ___ ___ ___ .

2. It is n ___ ___ ___ .

3. We have w ___ ___ ___ .

4. We all sit in a l ___ ___ ___ .

5. Our meal is div ___ ___ ___ .

THE ine FAMILY

dine	line	vine
divine	mine	whine
fine	nine	wine
	pine	

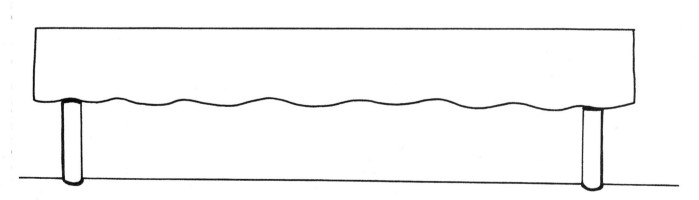

DoodleLoops

Fill in the missing letters in the *ing* family.
Then label the pictures.

w __ __ __

THE
ing
FAMILY

S __ __ __

br __ __ __   s __ __ __

cl __ __ __   sl __ __ __

fl __ __ __   str __ __ __

k __ __ __   th __ __ __

r __ __ __   w __ __ __

k __ __ __

r __ __ __

0-7682-3369-0 *Word Family DoodleLoops*

DoodleLoops

Fill in the missing letters.
You can find them in the house.
Then draw me.

1. I am a Th ___ ___ ___ .

2. I have one w ___ ___ ___ .

3. I wear a r ___ ___ ___ .

4. I am the K ___ ___ ___

   of all Things .

5. I love to s ___ ___ ___ .

THE
ing
FAMILY

bring	King	string
cling	ring	Thing
fling	sing	wing
	sling	

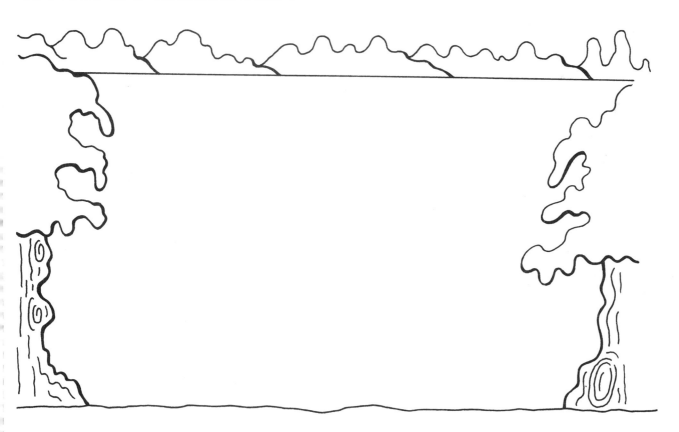

Fill in the missing letters in the *ore* family.

Then label the pictures.

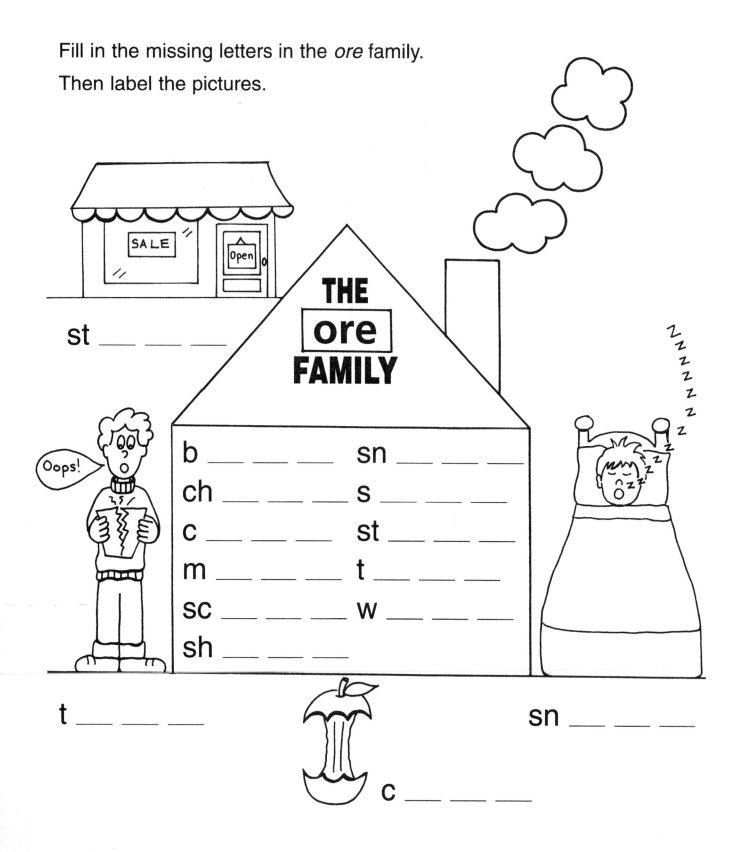

st ___ ___ ___

THE | **ore** | **FAMILY**

b ___ ___ ___   sn ___ ___ ___
ch ___ ___ ___   s ___ ___ ___
c ___ ___ ___   st ___ ___ ___
m ___ ___ ___   t ___ ___ ___
sc ___ ___ ___   w ___ ___ ___
sh ___ ___ ___

t ___ ___ ___

c ___ ___ ___

sn ___ ___ ___

0-7682-3369-0 *Word Family DoodleLoops*

DoodleLoops

Fill in the missing letters.
You can find them in the house.
Then draw me by my store.

THE ore FAMILY

bore	score	store
chore	shore	tore
core	snore	wore
more	sore	

1. I sit by the sh __ __ __ .

2. There is no one at

   my st __ __ __ .

3. This is really a b __ __ __ .

4. I begin to sn __ __ __ .

5. I want to do m __ __ __ .

0-7682-3369-0 *Word Family DoodleLoops*

DoodleLoops

Fill in the missing letters in the *ot* family.

Then label the pictures.

p __ __

kn __ __

THE
ot
FAMILY

bl __ __   n __ __

cl __ __   pl __ __

c __ __   p __ __

d __ __   r __ __

g __ __   sh __ __

h __ __   sl __ __

j __ __   sp __ __

kn __ __   t __ __

l __ __   tr __ __

h __ __

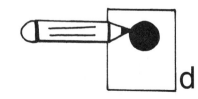

d __ __

t __ __

0-7682-3369-0 *Word Family DoodleLoops*

DoodleLoops

Fill in the missing letters.
You can find them in the house.
Then draw us.

1. I am a t ___ ___ .

2. I am very h___ ___ .

3. I am on a c ___ ___ .

4. I am getting a sh ___ ___ .

5. I g ___ ___ the chicken pox.

THE ot FAMILY

blot	jot	rot
clot	knot	shot
cot	lot	slot
dot	not	spot
got	plot	tot
hot	pot	trot

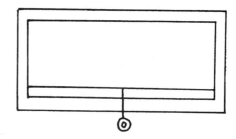

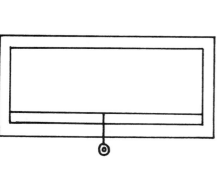

DoodleLoops

Fill in the missing letters in the *ow* family.
Then label the pictures.

scarecr ___ ___

r ___ ___

THE OW FAMILY

bl ___ ___   l ___ ___
b ___ ___   m ___ ___
cr ___ ___   sh ___ ___
fl ___ ___   sl ___ ___
gl ___ ___   sn ___ ___
gr ___ ___   r ___ ___
kn ___ ___   t ___ ___

bl ___ ___

b ___ ___

sn ___ ___

0-7682-3369-0 *Word Family DoodleLoops*

DoodleLoops

Fill in the missing letters.
You can find them in the house.
Then draw us.

1. We stand in a r ___ ___ .

2. We move very sl ___ ___ .

3. We gr ___ ___ very tired !

4. The moon has a bright

gl ___ ___ .

5. The wind starts to bl ___ ___ .

THE OW FAMILY

blow	grow	show
bow	know	slow
crow	low	snow
flow	mow	tow
glow	row	

DoodleLoops

Fill in the missing letters in the *un* family.

Then label the pictures.

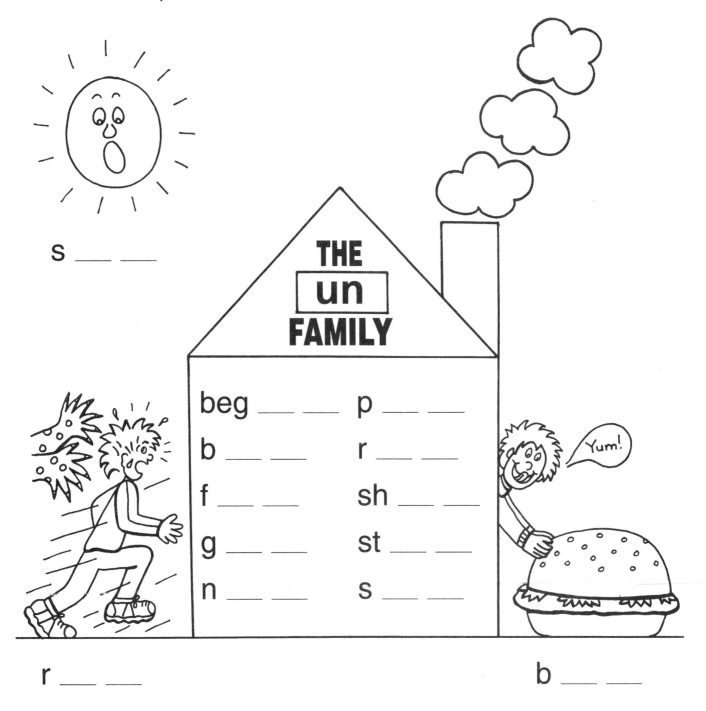

s ___ ___

THE **un** **FAMILY**

beg ___ ___   p ___ ___ ___

b ___ ___ ___   r ___ ___ ___

f ___ ___ ___   sh ___ ___ ___

g ___ ___ ___   st ___ ___ ___

n ___ ___ ___   s ___ ___ ___

Yum!

r ___ ___   b ___ ___

DoodleLoops

Fill in the missing letters.
You can find them in the house.
Then draw me.

1. I am having f ___ ___ .

2. I have a squirt g ___ ___ .

3. I r ___ ___ and r ___ ___ .

4. I am lying in the s ___ ___ .

5. I am eating a hot dog

on a b ___ ___ .

THE un FAMILY

begun	gun	shun
bun	nun	stun
fun	pun	sun
	run	

DoodleLoops

Fill in the missing letters in the y family.

Then label the pictures.

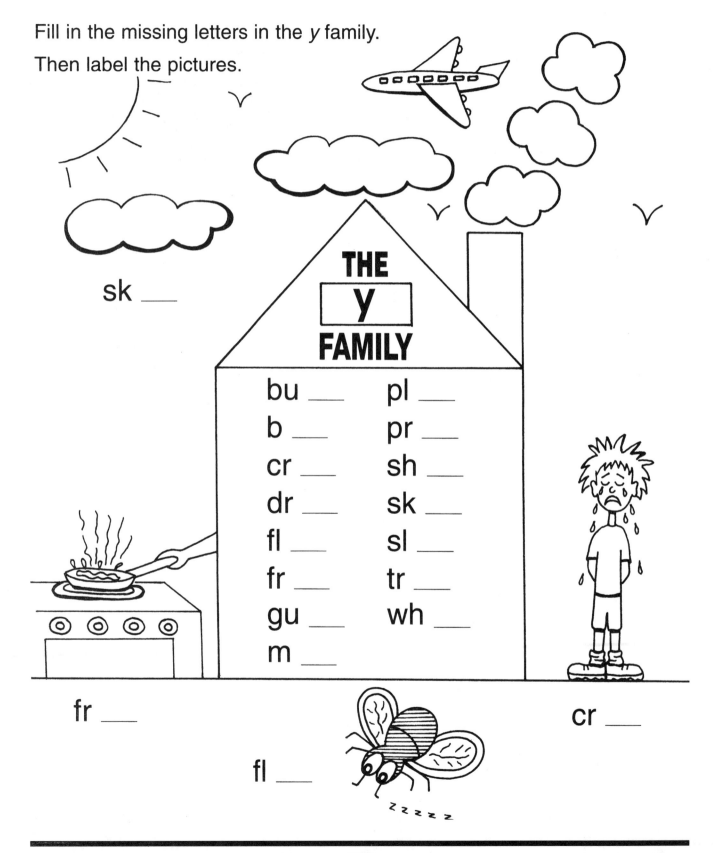

sk ___

THE
y
FAMILY

bu ___	pl ___
b ___	pr ___
cr ___	sh ___
dr ___	sk ___
fl ___	sl ___
fr ___	tr ___
gu ___	wh ___
m ___	

fr ___

cr ___

fl ___

Published by Frank Schaffer Publications. Copyright protected.
0-7682-3369-0 Word Family DoodleLoops

DoodleLoops

Fill in the missing letters.
You can find them in the house.
Then draw yourself and the guy
in the sky.

1. I am a gu ____ .

2. I know how to fl ____ .

3. I'm way up in the sk ____ .

4. Wh ____ don't you tr ____ ?

5. Come on! Don't be sh ____ !

THE
Y
FAMILY

DOODLE
LOOPS

buy	fry	shy
by	guy	sky
cry	my	sly
dry	ply	try
fly	pry	Why

_____   _____

_____   _____

_____   _____

_____   _____

_____   _____

_____   _____

_____   _____

_____   _____

_____   _____

_____   _____

_____   _____

_____   _____